Keys to Elevate

Demond Hicks

Copyright © 2023 by Demond Hicks

All rights reserved.

No part of this book may be reproduced in any form or by any electronic or mechanical means, including information storage and retrieval systems, without written permission from the author, except for the use of brief quotations in a book review.

Contents

Introduction   v

1. Environment   1
2. Positive Thinking   10
3. Intentional Action   18

Introduction

So many of my friends have reached out asking for guidance. One particular friend reached out to me and said, "I'm tryna change my mindset, but it's hard for me to do that. How did you do it?" That caught me off-guard, which inspired me to write this book called *KEYS to Elevate*--three short, powerful chapters consisting of my personal experiences, methods, principles, and tactics I implemented to elevate.

Chapter 1
Environment

We all have heard the quote, "Hang around 3 millionaires, and you will be the 4th." How many times has that gone over your head? Another quote we've all heard is "Show me your friends, and I'll show you your future." These quotes sound so cliche, but I promise they are not. The last 7 years of my life proved that. When I was 16, I had a best friend that I would hang out with everyday. The environments where we would hang and the people we would surround ourselves with did not align with what I felt I wanted out of life.

The day I realized that is the day I stopped putting myself in those environments. But my best friend did not, and let's just say that today he and I are in two different places in life. Moving forward in life, I started to surround myself with individuals who wanted more out of life, whose goals aligned with mine. I learned that hanging with people you have something in common with will easily motivate you.

Isn't it funny how life works? You think it should be easy to understand that, but in life sometimes your best judgment is blinded, or you may just need a little guidance. I read in a book by an author named Jim Rohn that says that if you wanna lose weight, get around individuals who are in the process of losing weight or have already lost weight.

These years of understanding this logic have elevated my life in a major way. In the year 2021, I decided I wanted my life to reach another level financially, so I decided to implement those same tools once again. I reached out to my mentor, who is a very well established, successful Black man, someone who I know could help me reach the financial level I was aiming for. I asked him if I could hang with him more often, and of course he said yes.

Those following weeks, I explained to him how I wanted to increase my income, which in those following weeks of me hanging with him my income surely did. Surrounding myself with someone who has so much valuable information and knowledge on financial literacy helped me get to my destination a little quicker. It's about the environment and the people you surround yourself with. Never ever forget that if you wanna be GREAT, hang with great people. If you wanna be a loser, well... you know what to do.

Principles of Changing Your Environment:

1. Set clear goals: Identify what you want to achieve by changing your environment, and make sure your goals are specific, measurable, achievable, relevant, and time-bound.
2. Create a plan: Once you have clear goals, develop a plan of action to achieve them. This may include breaking your goals down into smaller steps, identifying potential obstacles and how to overcome them, and creating a timeline for your actions.
3. Take action: Implement your plan by taking action towards your goals. This may involve making changes to your physical surroundings, your daily routine, your habits, or your relationships.
4. Monitor and adjust: Monitor your progress regularly and adjust your plan as necessary. Reflect on what is working well and what isn't, and make changes accordingly.

Environment

5. Seek support: Seek support from others who can help you achieve your goals, such as friends, family, colleagues, or professionals. This may involve asking for advice, accountability, or emotional support.

Benefits of Changing Your Environment:

1. Increased motivation: Changing your environment can create a sense of excitement and motivation, as you are taking active steps towards your goals.
2. Improved productivity: By creating a more conducive environment, you may find that you are able to work more efficiently and effectively.
3. Reduced stress: A change in environment can help to reduce stress by creating a more comfortable and peaceful space, or by eliminating sources of stress.
4. Enhanced creativity: A new environment can inspire creativity and new ideas, as you are exposed to different stimuli and perspectives.
5. Personal growth: Changing your environment can be a powerful tool for personal growth, as it can help you to develop new skills, overcome challenges, and build resilience.

Keys to Elevate

1. What changes do you want to make to your environment to better support your personal growth and development?
2. What are some habits or behaviors that you need to eliminate from your environment to better align with your goals and values?
3. How can you create a physical space that supports your productivity, creativity, or overall well-being?
4. What relationships or social circles do you need to reevaluate to better support your personal growth and development?
5. How can you incorporate intentional action and positive thinking into your environment to support your personal growth and development?

Chapter 2
Positive Thinking

Positive thinking is so tricky since anything could trigger negative thoughts. I want to share a favorite quote of mine: "Life doesn't happen *to* you, it happens *for* you." I wanna share another quote, this one by J Prince: "There are two things you get everyday...a Chance and a Choice." These are quotes I wish I had heard earlier in life. In the year 2020, I lost my job, and as a young father, I almost panicked. But I knew better than to think negatively about it. Realizing that thinking negative would do nothing but make me feel worse. Once I decided to switch my outlook on the situation, I was able to think cleaer. That allowed me to put the right effort towards finding a better job, and guess what? I did.

Like I said before, positive thinking is so tricky since anything could trigger negative thoughts. I wanna ask you a question: when you wake up in the morning, what is the first thing you think about--the problems from yesterday or the new opportunities for today? My goal has been to keep myself in a positive mindset. What's that old question people ask? "Is the glass half empty or half full?" I wanna be the person who doesn't have to think twice about answering that question. The glass is half full.

Positive Thinking

Principles of Positive Thinking:

1. Practice gratitude: Cultivate a mindset of gratitude by focusing on what you have rather than what you lack. This can help to shift your perspective and foster a sense of abundance and positivity.
2. Reframe negative thoughts: Train yourself to reframe negative thoughts in a more positive light. For example, instead of saying "I can't do this," say "I will try my best and learn from my mistakes."
3. Focus on solutions: Rather than dwelling on problems, focus on finding solutions. This can help to shift your mindset from a negative to a proactive and problem-solving one.
4. Surround yourself with positivity: Surround yourself with positive people, activities, and environments that support your positive thinking efforts.
5. Practice self-care: Take care of your physical and emotional well-being by practicing self-care activities such as exercise, meditation, and self-reflection.

Benefits of Positive Thinking:

1. Improved mental health: Positive thinking can help to reduce symptoms of anxiety and depression, and improve overall mental health.
2. Increased resilience: A positive mindset can help you to bounce back from challenges and setbacks more easily.
3. Improved relationships: Positive thinking can improve your relationships with others by fostering a more compassionate and empathetic attitude.
4. Increased motivation: A positive mindset can help to increase motivation and productivity, as you approach challenges with a can-do attitude.

Keys to Elevate

5. Improved physical health: Positive thinking can also have physical health benefits, such as lower blood pressure and reduced risk of heart disease.

---

1. What negative thoughts or beliefs do you want to work on reframing into more positive ones?
2. What are some things that you feel grateful for in your life, and how can you practice gratitude regularly?
3. What self-talk can you use to replace negative self-talk when it arises?
4. What are some positive people, activities, or environments that you can surround yourself with to support positive thinking?
5. What self-care activities can you practice to improve your overall well-being and cultivate a positive mindset?

Chapter 3
Intentional Action

Intentional means "on purpose" and action means "the fact or process of doing something." Imagine wanting more out of life but not doing anything to get more out of life. I remember listening to motivational videos some years back, and while listening to them, I felt I was getting things done. I know. That sounds delusional, right? Well, what I didn't realize then was that the time that I wasted listening to those motivational videos, I could be putting in intentional action towards my dreams and goals.

Year 2021 is the year I officially took intentional action. A very good friend of mine told me they did not wanna hear about my dreams anymore--they wanted to see them be

put into action. The day that happened, I had to ask myself what it is that I want. The first thing I did was write down all the things that I wanted to accomplish, then write down the steps I had to take to see them manifest. At this point, I

wasn't being delusional. I was being intentional.

Intentional Action

After taking the necessary steps that I needed I literally saw all the things I wrote down manifest. It's amazing how far you can get in life with a little bit of planning and proper action.

Again, all the things I've talked about could seem simple or seem complex, but these are my Keys to Elevating-- Environment, Positive Thinking, and Intentional Action.

I challenge you to grow in those three areas. You won't regret it.

Principles of Intentional Action:

1. Identify your values and goals: Take the time to identify your personal values and goals, and use these as a guide for intentional action.
2. Plan and prioritize: Create a plan of action and prioritize tasks based on their importance and alignment with your values and goals.
3. Stay focused: Stay focused on your goals and avoid distractions by setting boundaries and eliminating unnecessary activities.
4. Take action consistently: Take action consistently towards your goals, even if it means taking small steps each day.
5. Reflect and adjust: Reflect on your progress regularly and adjust your actions as necessary to ensure they are aligned with your values and goals.

Benefits of Intentional Action:

1. Greater sense of purpose: Intentional action can help you to identify and pursue your personal values and goals, which can lead to a greater sense of purpose in life.
2. Increased productivity: By prioritizing tasks and eliminating distractions, intentional action can help you to work more efficiently and increase productivity.

Keys to Elevate

3. Improved decision-making: Intentional action can help you to make better decisions by aligning your actions with your values and goals.
4. Enhanced self-awareness: Intentional action can also increase self-awareness by helping you to understand your personal values, strengths, and weaknesses.
5. Reduced stress: Intentional action can help to reduce stress by providing a sense of control and purpose, and by reducing feelings of overwhelm and anxiety associated with uncertainty and lack of direction.

---

1. What personal values and goals do you have that you want to prioritize with intentional action?
2. What is one area of your life where you feel like you could benefit from taking more intentional action?
3. What habits or activities do you need to eliminate or prioritize to better align with your values and goals?
4. How can you stay focused on your goals and avoid distractions?
5. What steps will you take to ensure you are taking consistent action towards your goals, and how will you track your progress and adjust as necessary?

Win in real life!